For my daughters—Jaime, Maya, and Leila—
all three, Bold, Brave, and Beautiful
—L. C.-R.

For Eileen. You're a sunny day.
—R. C.

SIMON & SCHUSTER BOOKS FOR YOUNG READERS
An imprint of Simon & Schuster Children's Publishing Division
1230 Avenue of the Americas, New York, New York 10020
Text copyright © 2019 by Lesa Cline-Ransome
Illustrations copyright © 2019 by Raúl Colón
All rights reserved, including the right of reproduction in whole or in part in any form.
SIMON & SCHUSTER BOOKS FOR YOUNG READERS is a trademark of Simon & Schuster, Inc.
For information about special discounts for bulk purchases, please contact Simon & Schuster Special Sales
at 1-866-506-1949 or business@simonandschuster.com.
The Simon & Schuster Speakers Bureau can bring authors to your live event. For more information or to book an event,
contact the Simon & Schuster Speakers Bureau at 1-866-248-3049 or visit our website at www.simonspeakers.com.
Book design by Laurent Linn
The text for this book was set in Geometric 415 BT.
The illustrations for this book are rendered in watercolors, Prismacolor pencils, and lithograph pencils on Arches paper.
Manufactured in China
0821 SCP
4 6 8 10 9 7 5 3
Library of Congress Cataloging-in-Publication Data
Names: Cline-Ransome, Lesa, author. | Colón, Raúl, illustrator.
Title: Counting the stars / Lesa Cline-Ransome ; illustrated by Raúl Colón.
Description: First edition. | New York : Simon & Schuster Books for Young Readers, [2019] |
"A Paula Wiseman Book." | Audience: Age 4–8. | Audience: K to grade 3.
Identifiers: LCCN 2018039827 | ISBN 9781534404755 (hardcover) | ISBN 9781534404762 (eBook)
Subjects: LCSH: Johnson, Katherine G.—Juvenile literature. | United States. National Aeronautics and Space Administration—Biography—Juvenile literature. |
African American women mathematicians—Biography—Juvenile literature. | Women mathematicians—Biography—Juvenile literature. |
African American women—Biography—Juvenile literature.
Classification: LCC QA29.J64 C55 2019 | DDC 510.92 [B]—dc23
LC record available at https://lccn.loc.gov/2018039827

WOMEN & SCIENCE

COUNTING THE STARS

Lesa Cline-Ransome

Illustrated by Raúl Colón

A Paula Wiseman Book
SIMON & SCHUSTER BOOKS FOR YOUNG READERS
New York London Toronto Sydney New Delhi

Katherine Johnson was born the fourth child of Joshua and Joylette Coleman and the first to love numbers.

By the time Katherine could speak, she was counting. She even counted the steps she walked from her front porch to Sunday morning church service. At night, after her mama and daddy tucked her into bed and the moon shone bright in the West Virginia sky, Katherine counted the stars, one by one.

She was too young to go to school, so Katherine followed behind her sister and brothers to the two-room schoolhouse in White Sulphur Springs. When the teacher noticed the tiny, curly-haired girl reading along with other students, she offered Katherine her own seat.

Her mother was a teacher, but it was her father, a lumberman and farmer, who could figure numbers in his head faster than anyone Katherine knew.

Why? What? How? Her father helped her find the answers to her math questions when her teachers couldn't. At six years old, instead of starting her first day in kindergarten, Katherine went straight to second grade. Instead of starting third grade, Katherine went to fifth.

During the school year, Joshua and Joylette left behind their farm and rented a home 125 miles away in Institute, West Virginia, and enrolled all four Coleman children in school at West Virginia Institute. Joshua traveled back and forth, working as a bellman to make ends meet. The Colemans' sacrifice paid off, and by the time Katherine was ten, she started her first year of high school in Institute.

When Katherine wasn't outdoors with friends or exploring her own backyard, she spent her time alone indoors where the world she explored existed only in her own imagination.

In the early evenings, Katherine's principal walked his youngest student home, stopping to point out the constellations overhead. Ever since she had counted stars outside her bedroom window at night, Katherine's mind swirled with questions that soared past the clouds and far beyond Earth.

In 1933, with high school ending and the Great Depression beginning, Katherine wondered if she could find more answers in college. But with times tough all over, college seemed as far away as the moon. However, West Virginia State Institute found promise in the fifteen-year-old with a gift for numbers and offered her a full scholarship. She entered the college's math department.

As she walked across campus, numbers would march in Katherine's head. Calculus, algebra, trigonometry, probability classes—Katherine took them all. When her college ran out of classes for Katherine to take, her math professor, William Claytor, created an analytic geometry course just for her. All alone, she sat in a classroom with empty seats behind her, chalkboards filled with mathematical proofs and formulas in front of her.

"You would make a good research mathematician," Professor Claytor told her.

Katherine knew a lot of girls in the segregated South who were teachers, mothers, and nurses, but she had never met one who was a mathematician.

"But where will I find a job?" Katherine asked.

Professor Claytor continued scribbling numbers on the board and said, "That will be your problem."

When college ended, teaching began for Katherine at a high school in West Virginia where she was nearly as young as her students. Outside of the classroom, Katherine found love in the brown eyes and big heart of Jimmy Goble. She loved teaching as much as she loved Jimmy, but in 1940s West Virginia, married women weren't allowed in the classroom. So, quickly and quietly, the two became one.

They both now taught at a high school in Jimmy's hometown of Marion, Virginia. First one, then two, then three daughters were born. Two teacher's salaries plus two summer jobs barely equaled a roof over their heads. And with three little girls to care for, Katherine and Jimmy knew the numbers weren't adding up. Jimmy's sister and brother-in-law told them of the opportunities in Hampton, Virginia, where there were plenty of shipyard jobs waiting for Jimmy and even a government job for Katherine. It wasn't teaching, but over at the National Advisory Committee for Aeronautics at Langley Aeronautics, word was they were looking for women who were good with numbers for their computing department.

"Let's do it," Katherine decided. She didn't know much about flight, but Katherine knew an awful lot about math.

Dorothy Vaughn, a ten-year veteran at Langley, greeted Katherine on her first day as a human "computer" in the Aircraft Loads Building at Langley Aeronautics. The West Computing office was filled with the brown faces of women furiously completing data sheets of equations. Dorothy knew Katherine's family back in White Sulphur Springs and she knew Katherine's reputation with numbers.

Nearly twenty years earlier when the computing pool began, many of the engineers wondered aloud how the female mind could possibly process concepts as complicated as math. But it was the job of these women computers to double-check the engineers' data, develop complex equations, and analyze the numbers. Each desk had a calculating machine, but many of the women didn't need them.

Katherine had barely settled into the routine at Langley when Dorothy called her and a coworker over to her desk.

"The Flight Research Division is requesting two new computers," Dorothy told them. "I'm sending you two." It was just a temporary assignment, she told them, two weeks at the most.

Katherine grabbed her purse and hurried over to Building 1244, curious to see what the engineers were up to. Outside the Research Division building, a runway was humming with aircraft. Inside, the office hummed with energy. Katherine found a seat and got to work.

She ignored the stares and the COLORED GIRLS signs on the bathroom door and the segregated cafeteria, eating instead at her desk. Katherine ignored all of it, and did what she was hired to do: make the numbers work.

Katherine asked questions over the engineers' shoulders as they worked, read their issues of *Aviation Week* till her eyes were strained. Why? What? How?

From her first assignment, Katherine's flawless analysis and in-depth research made her a favorite. Her desk was piled high with requests for numbers to crunch as her two-week temporary assignment doubled, then tripled. After six months it was clear: Katherine was a permanent part of the team.

When the engineers went to meetings to discuss research behind closed doors, Katherine asked to go. "Girls don't go to meetings," she was told.

But again and again, Katherine continued to ask to attend until she got the answer she wanted: Yes.

Now Katherine sat at the table in the meetings, the only woman, the only computer, the only brown face, taking notes as engineers discussed new discoveries and machine computers that worked fifteen times faster than humans. Katherine listened even closer when they began discussing a brand-new field—space.

On October 4, 1957, the Soviet Union launched *Sputnik*, the first artificial satellite to orbit the Earth. *Sputnik* may have beaten the United States into outer space, but the race was far from over. The National Advisory Committee for Aeronautics changed its focus from airplanes when it became the National Aeronautics and Space Administration, NASA. The race to space was in full swing.

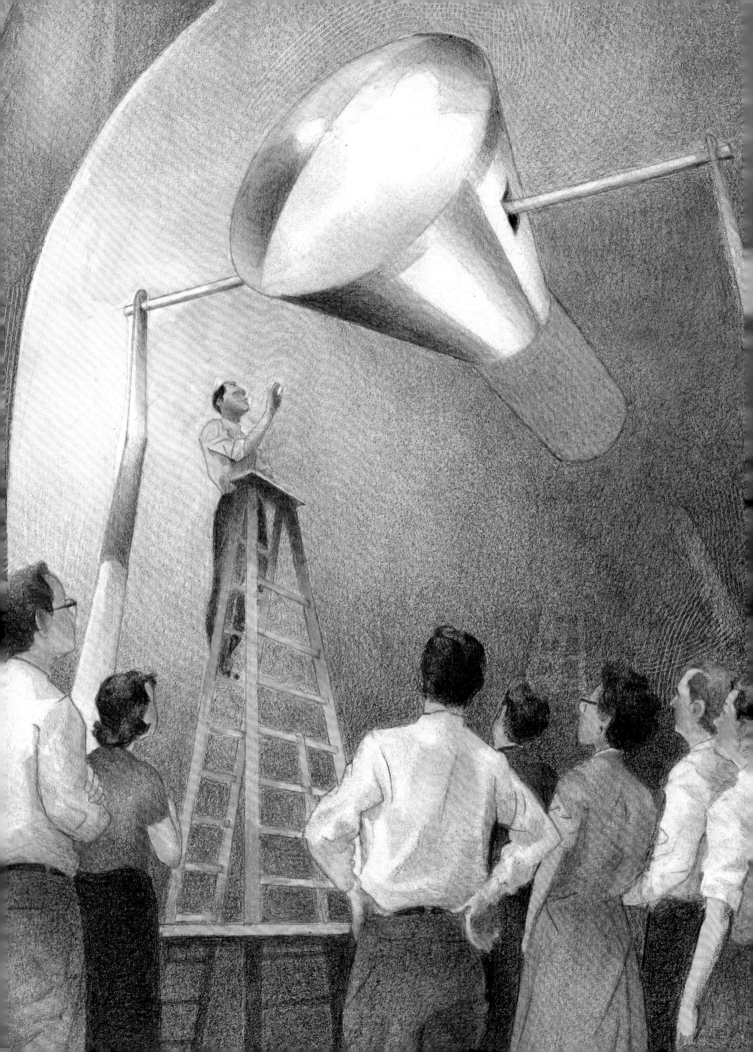

The long hours Katherine's team worked grew longer as the US hurried to find an answer to the Soviet Union's *Sputnik*. They found it just a few months later when they launched the *Explorer 1* satellite. The more space discoveries there were, the more the world wanted to know. The bleeps and signals from the satellites orbiting Earth transmitted to radios in homes across the country made people wonder how much more was beyond Earth's atmosphere. Was there life on other planets? Could man travel into space?

NASA set out to answer those questions with Project Mercury. Named for the Roman god of travel, the *Mercury*, a six-foot-wide spacecraft, would carry the first man into Earth's orbit. They just needed to figure out how. Engineers ran over one million experiments, test runs, simulations, and inspections, and still in 1961 the Russians again beat the United States when their first human shot into space orbited Earth.

The US grew tired of waiting. Why weren't we winning the space race? The folks at NASA had the best minds, the skills, expensive computers. They had Mercury Seven, a group of experienced NASA-trained pilots. They even had a secret weapon—Katherine Johnson.

It was the engineers' job to plot the path of the spacecraft from the moment it left the launchpad until the moment of its descent into the Atlantic Ocean. The Mercury-Atlas rocket would thrust the three-thousand-pound, eleven-foot capsule up into the air with enough force to orbit the Earth, but the tricky part, they all knew, wasn't getting the astronaut launched. It was getting him back.

"Let me do it," Katherine told the head engineer. "Tell me where you want the man to land, and I'll tell you where to send him up."

Huddled at their desks, Katherine and the engineers came up with a few different equations for trajectories or possible outcomes to program into the computers, knowing that one wrong number, one wrong decimal, could mean the difference between success and failure, life and death.

With the stars glowing outside her window, Katherine spent her nights awake and her days at a chalkboard. Questions and numbers once again swirled in her head, but this time she was calculating distances, plotting trajectories, and noting the Earth's gravity and speed of rotation, making sure the flight was a success for NASA and the astronaut, John Glenn.

With the flight crew, spacecraft, and launch team all ready to go, John Glenn was not. He needed one final check of the computer's calculations. He needed Katherine.

"Call her," he told the engineers. "Get the girl to check the numbers."

Katherine had one and a half days before launch day to double-check the trajectory numbers that a mechanical computer had taken just hours to spit out. She worked each digit backward and forward. When finally her numbers and the computer's were a perfect match, John Glenn was ready to go.

10-9-8-7-6-5-4-3-2-1 . . . BLAST OFF!

On February 20, 1962, Katherine watched the broadcast as the Mercury-Atlas rocket boosted John Glenn into history as the first American to orbit Earth. Katherine counted as she watched the screen—three orbits, four hours, fifty-five minutes, and twenty-three seconds until finally John Glenn and the capsule splashed down safely in the Atlantic Ocean.

As the world cheered, Katherine wondered. *Why? What? How* could she make numbers take an astronaut even farther, beyond Earth's atmosphere and maybe even to the moon?

KATHERINE JOHNSON was born on August 26, 1918, in White Sulphur Springs, West Virginia. Growing up in the segregated South, Katherine never dreamed that as an African-American woman she would one day play an integral role in shaping the history of the space program.

"Everything was so new—the whole idea of going into space was new and daring."

Her father, Joshua Coleman, had received only a sixth-grade education, but he instilled in all his children a love of learning and in his youngest daughter, Katherine, a keen interest in math.

"I had a very, very interesting childhood, but, oh my, education was the primary focus in our family."

In college, her professor and mentor William Schieffelin Claytor, an esteemed mathematician who received his PhD from the University of Pennsylvania, created advanced, customized courses for Katherine and she graduated with highest honors in 1937.

After several years teaching high school math, Katherine became the first black woman to integrate West Virginia University's graduate math program in 1940.

Katherine began working at Langley's Flight Research Division in 1953, where she spent the start of her career as a computer, analyzing data from flight tests and becoming the first woman to coauthor a research report in the Flight Division at NASA.

In 1961, it was Katherine who did the trajectory analysis for America's first human space flight for astronaut Alan Shepard Jr. The following year, when *Friendship 7* launched John Glenn into space as the first astronaut to orbit Earth, she hand calculated the numbers for his flight path. But one of Katherine's proudest moments was being part of the team that launched the rocket for Apollo 11, by calculating the flight path astronauts Neil Armstrong, Buzz Aldrin, and Michael Collins used to make the world's first moon landing.

"I was just excited to have challenging work to do and smart people to work with," Katherine said of her time at NASA. In 1986 Katherine retired after thirty-three years of service.

In 2015 Katherine received the Presidential Medal of Freedom, the nation's highest civilian honor, from President Barack Obama.

Katherine's pivotal role at NASA was highlighted in Margot Lee Shetterly's book *Hidden Figures*, which became a major motion picture in 2016. Her character was portrayed by award-winning actress Taraji P. Henson. Katherine, at age ninety-eight, encouraged all young people to see the film, saying, "It will give a more positive outlook on what is possible if you work, do your best, and are prepared."

Lesa Cline-Ransome